Your church is a miracle. If you didn't know that, this book will help you understand why. Both new believers and old believers with conflicted feelings about the church will especially benefit. Read this excellent book to learn how to love Christ's people better and worship God more.

Jonathan Leeman, Editorial Director, 9Marks

This book about the church is a gift to the church. It's clear, winsome, and needed, reminding us of the great reality of the body of Christ called to live, worship, and minister together in his name until he comes. I'm grateful for this biblical call to remember who we are, and what by God's mercy we get to be and do as his gathered people.

Kathleen Nielson, Director of Women's Initiatives at The Gospel Coalition

An excellent and hugely important book. Up-to-date, punchy, and humorous but penetrating. Sam makes the case that we need to re-discover the huge relevance of the church in our Christian lives.

Terry Virgo, founder of Newfrontiers

We couldn't be more excited about this book. Especially in our day when people look for reasons to reject the church, this book is a necessary encouragement. Sam expertly engages readers with what the Bible says, and brings the truth home through illustrations that stick with you. We're eager to see church members, ministers, and cross-cultural workers benefit from "Why Bother With Church?".

Dave and Gloria Furman: Pastor, Redeemer Church of Dubai; author of *The Pastor's Wife*

This is a thoroughly enjoyable book. It ably addresses many questions people are asking about the church. Without minimising its flaws, Sam helps us see that the church is a miracle of grace, destined for eternal glory as the bride of Christ. Sam has a God-given gift for presenting complex topics in ways that are biblically faithful, skilfully concise, pastorally wise, and culturally relevant.

Bob Kauflin, Director of Sovereign Grace Music

I'm so glad Sam wrote this book. Many in our day say that they like Jesus, but not the church. But is it possible to belong to the Head without being part of his visible body? This is a wise, winsome invitation to embrace the riches of communion with Christ's new society.

**Michael Horton, Professor of Theology,
Westminster Seminary, California**

Why bother with church?

And other questions about why you
need it and why it needs you

Sam Allberry

Questions
Christians ask

Why bother with church?
And other questions about why you need it and why it needs you
© Sam Allberry/The Good Book Company, 2016. Reprinted 2016.

Published by
The Good Book Company
Tel (UK): 0333 123 0880
Tel (North America): (1) 866 244 2165
International: +44 (0) 208 942 0880
Email (UK): info@thegoodbook.co.uk
Email (North America): info@thegoodbook.com

Websites
UK & Europe: www.thegoodbook.co.uk
North America: www.thegoodbook.com
Australia: www.thegoodbook.com.au
New Zealand: www.thegoodbook.co.nz

the good book
COMPANY

ISBN: 9781909559141

Printed in Denmark
Design by André Parker

Contents

To the church family at St Mary's

The park or the church?

Being honest, on some Sundays, the park looked like a better option.

I was working for a church in Oxford, and my walk to the morning service every Sunday took me through a park. It was lovely. There was something for everyone: a swimming pool, tennis courts, a boating pond, a lake full of ducks, a playground, plenty of space for ball games and plenty of benches for watching everyone doing their something. On a sunny Sunday morning the place was full: everyone doing their thing and having a great time.

And there I was, walking through it all, Bible tucked under my arm, on my way to church. And the question was: If I wasn't a pastor, would I stop? If my pay cheque didn't kind of depend on my being at church, would I stay in the park?

The park looked like a lot less effort than the church. It didn't look as if anyone in the park was going to put me on a rota. No one was going to ask me to pick up the tennis balls every other Sunday, or turn up early to get the ducks out.

The park looked like a lot of fun. You could choose what you wanted to do, how often you went, if you went, and how long you stayed. Feel like tennis? Come and play. Feel more like sitting on your own reading a book? Great. And if you're not here next week, that's fine. You can make friends, or not, as you wish.

The park also looked a lot more normal. No one would think I was strange for going there. Lots of my friends might like to come. Going to the park is a regular, normal part of 21st-century life.

Church, increasingly, isn't.

I am sure I am not the only Christian (and not the only pastor) to have had these feelings. Many if not most of us have our own equivalent to the park. We live in a time when there is a huge number of alternatives to church on a Sunday, readily available and seemingly very attractive. Sports. Bed. Shopping. Brunch with the gang. Hobbies. And as the number of options available to us grows and grows, church seems more and more irrelevant than ever.

In the UK, it was normal to go to church back in the 1950s—25% of British adults were in a service on a Sunday. Today, it's 5%. It's likely that more people will be in your local supermarket at 11 a.m. this Sunday than in your local church. In the US, that trend, though less far on, is nevertheless heading in the same direction.

There are so many reasons why we might not bother with church.

Church is an effort. It is sometimes hard. And it's far from normal. So why bother going at all? Why bother making it a priority in your week, every week? Why bother getting stuck in when it means putting yourself out? After all, the park is right there, ready and waiting.

That's what this book is about. Maybe you're someone who goes along dutifully to church week by week, but you've never been completely sure why. Maybe you're stuck in and serving hard, but wondering if it's all worth the effort. Maybe you're someone whose commitment to church has been waning for a while now. Or maybe you're new to church and you want to know what it is that you're getting into.

Whoever you are, I hope you'll find this book realistic and useful. I hope that you'll grow not just to be bothered, but excited about your church. This book's last line will be:

*Why on earth would I **not** bother with church?*

You may feel a long way away from thinking that, and wondering how on earth you could ever get to that from where you are. Well, that's what the next 80 pages are about. But for now, let me sum it up in two words: what and whose.

When we get *what* the church is, and *whose* the church is, we really won't want to go to the park (or anywhere else) on Sunday morning.

If we don't, we won't...

9

Chapter 1

What is church?

For a number of years, I played tennis every Sunday morning with a good friend of mine. Giving up my lie-in, I'd walk to the end of my street where he'd pick me up at the same time each week, and we'd head to the local tennis club, whack a few balls around, catch up on each other's news and play a few sets until it started raining, someone else wanted the court, or my wildly inaccurate first serves had lost all our balls.

Then I became a Christian, and started going to my local church. Occasionally my tennis partner—now my ex-tennis partner, I suppose—would come with me. Ever since, Sunday mornings have meant church. A few years into my Christian life I started working for a church, so it also became part of my job to go. But even allowing for holidays and sickness, I can think of hardly any Sundays in the last twenty years when I didn't go to church.

Some might say my Sunday routine didn't change much. I just swapped one hobby for another. After all, I still give up my lie-in. I still head out at the same time each week, and still meet with a group of friends, where—among other things—we still catch up on each other's news.

It's easy to think of church as being a meeting place for those whose hobby happens to be God. On the surface, my church is a lot like my old tennis club: people meeting together because of a shared interest, running occasional events to raise the profile in the wider community, trying to drum up more members, having meetings with minutes and secretaries, and getting caught up in the minutiae of it all to a degree that would baffle most outsiders. There's also a lot of serving...

But scratch under the surface and there's a lot more going on.

The word "church" is so familiar to many today that we don't tend to stop and think about what we mean by it when we use it. A by-product of this is that we can easily and unwittingly end up actually misusing the word without realising it. Even before reading on, pause for a moment. Think of a sentence, or a few words, that sum up what you would say church is.

The church is a particular gathering

The word we commonly translate "church" in the New Testament is the Greek word *ecclesia*, which simply means "assembly" or "gathering". It was not a specifically religious word in New Testament times, and we see this reflected in the Bible itself. So in Acts 19, for instance, "ecclesia" is used twice. Neither refers to the meeting at Holy Trinity, Genericsville, at 10.30 on Sunday mornings. The writer, Luke, is recounting Paul's mission trip to Ephesus; and as Paul preached, he sparked off a riot. Luke describes the chaos of the crowd:

> The assembly was in confusion: some were shouting one thing, some another. Most of the people did not even know why they were there.
>
> *Acts 19 v 32*

A local clerk eventually intervenes to calm the crowd down. Among other things, he says to them:

> If, then, Demetrius and his fellow craftsmen have a grievance against anybody, the courts are open and there are proconsuls. They can press charges. If there is anything further you want to bring up, it must be settled in a legal assembly.
>
> *Acts 19 v 38-39*

In these two passages, Luke uses the word *ecclesia*. In one instance it refers to a riotous mob, in the other to a legal body. In both cases it simply describes the gathering of a group of people—a "church"—irrespective of their purpose and composition.

But as the early Christians maintained the habit of gathering regularly together, *ecclesia* came more and more to refer specifically to a Christian gathering—to the weekly meeting of believers to worship God and serve one another. In Acts 5 v 11, for example, Luke can write that "great fear seized the whole church" using this very same word.

The word has now been taken over by this Christian context for it. Many of the words that relate to church life are derived from *ecclesia*—"ecclesiology" describes the doctrine of the church that we find in the Bible, "ecclesiastical" refers to matters concerning to denominational or local church affairs, and so on.

Ecclesia being the New Testament word for church is a significant indication of what a church actually is in essence. A church is a particular gathering of Christian believers—of people who have heard Jesus' promise that in him, "the kingdom of God has come near" and obeyed Jesus' command to "repent and believe the good news" by accepting him as King of their life, and as trusting him as their Saviour who gives them eternal life (Mark 1 v 15). It is a *particular* gathering because it is clear from the Bible that any meeting of two or more Christians, whatever the context, does not constitute what the New Testament regards as church. Bumping into a Christian friend in a grocery store does not mean that this piece of human interaction in the ice-cream aisle is a church.

We can go further back in the Bible to see what it is that makes church such a distinctive way of meeting. Following his rescue of Israel from slavery in Egypt, God brought the people together at the foot of Mount Sinai. They camped in the wilderness there while Moses went up the mountain to meet with God (Exodus 19 v 1-6). It was during this time that God spoke to the Israelites as his chosen people, and identified them as uniquely belonging to him, commissioned for his service. God also gave them his law, by which they would live as his rescued people. This law served to define them and to teach them how they were to live out their status as his people.

The Bible later looks back on this gathering as being the prototype of church. New Testament writers referring to this time used that very same word *ecclesia* to describe what was happening at Sinai (see, for example, Acts 7 v 38; Stephen describes the gathering of God's people at Sinai as "the assembly"—literally, "the ecclesia"). At the foot of Sinai, the people of God were "churching" together. And churching here means more than just hanging out over a latte and catching up on the weekend sports results. This gathering was marked by being in the presence of God, receiving his words of promise and direction, and being constituted as his people. The weekly gathering of Christians that the New Testament describes as church is something of a re-enactment of this moment. Christians gather as the people of God to receive his word afresh, to be reconstituted and recommissioned as his. (What this actually involves we'll look at further on.)

The church is an outpost

These local, weekly meetings of God's people are not just rehearsing a key moment from the Old Testament; they are a local and time-bound expression of something that is universal and timeless. All of the people of God, from across the ages, constitute his church— what is sometimes referred to as the universal church.

Spiritually, Christian people are seated with Christ at the right hand of the Father (Ephesians 2 v 6). Wherever we happen to find ourselves on earth, we are part of a vast and timeless spiritual gathering, one that the gathering at Sinai was just the foretaste of:

> You have not come to a mountain that can be touched and that is burning with fire; to darkness, gloom and storm; to a trumpet blast or to such a voice speaking words that those who heard it begged that no further word be spoken to them ...
>
> But you have come to Mount Zion, to the city of the living God, the heavenly Jerusalem. You have come to thousands upon thousands of angels in joyful assembly, to the church of the firstborn, whose names are written in heaven. You have come to God, the Judge of all, to the spirits of the righteous made perfect, to Jesus the mediator of a new covenant. *Hebrews 12 v 18-19, 22-24a*

Our mountain is not physical and earthly, but heavenly. This is the universal church. In one sense, in Christ, we're already there—but in another sense, we're not there yet. And so the local church is an outpost of this ultimate church. When Paul addresses his letter to the Christians in Corinth, he writes "to the church of God in Corinth" (1 Corinthians 1 v 2). These believers happen to be in Corinth—that is their physical and earthly location. And so they constitute the "church of God" in that place.

Paul does not say that they are "part" of the church of God, as if the church of God is all the local churches collected up and put together. No, the local church is the church of God, in that particular locale. They are the embodiment in Corinth of the universal church. The church functions like an embassy of this new society that God is creating through Christ. Just as the US embassy in London is considered a part of US sovereign territory overseas in a foreign land, so the local church is a small part of heavenly territory in this world.

So the church is the gathering in a particular location of God's people, as his people, in his presence, to hear and respond to his word. Two things follow from this.

First, the church is not the building God's people happen to meet in. We commonly use the word that way ("That's a beautiful/imposing/crumbling church"), but it is not really being accurate to the Bible to do so. The church is not the building itself, but the people meeting there. People don't enter a church; the church enters a building. In fact, a specially designated building is not even essential. In parts of Africa, Christians meet week by week under a spreading tree. Others will meet in the open air or in someone's home.

Second, the church is not the denomination. I pastor a church that belongs to the Church of England. It is the denomination to which I happen to belong. There is much I like about the Church of England (though it is changing in ways that mean I like it much less than I used to), but its name is not one of them. It is a misnomer. It is an association of churches. Biblically speaking, it is not, as an organisation, a church in and of itself.

When denominational representatives speak on behalf of the organisation, they are not technically speaking for all the Christians in England, still less for all the local churches in England. A better name would be something like "The Anglican Denomination in England".

The church is a family and an embassy

In his letter to the pastor Timothy, Paul says that a church leader needs to be able to...

> ... manage his own family well ... If anyone does not know how to manage his own family, how can he take care of God's church?
>
> *1 Timothy 3 v 4-5*

Paul's point is simple: as a household is a biological family, so a church is a spiritual family. Later in the same passage Paul describes the church as "God's household" (1 Timothy 3 v 15).

The church is God's family. It is not those who have signed up to a human institution, or who find themselves in natural sympathy with Christian ethics and church life. It is those who have been brought into God's family through the reconciling work of his Son. When we were adopted by God as his children, we were adopted into his family—we became part of a familial community. When God draws people to himself, he draws them into family.

All families have likenesses, whether of physical features or particular mannerisms. One characteristic of the church is "truth". Later in his letter to Timothy,

Paul describes church in these terms: "The church of the living God, the pillar and foundation of the truth" (1 Timothy 3 v 15).

The way in which the church depends on the truth is obvious: it is the truth of God's word that brings the church into existence and shapes all that she is to be. But there is also a way in which God's truth depends on the church: not that the church approves or decides on what the truth is, but that the church is the means by which God's truth reaches into his world. The church is the earthly outlet for God's truth, the embassy that represents him. Christians are this individually too, of course. But it is through the church being church, rather than primarily through individual believers each separately doing their bit, that the truth is upheld and commended to a watching world.

This is one of the reasons why church matters so much. I once heard it said that there is no such thing as a God-forsaken place (given that God is present everywhere), but there is such a thing as a church-forsaken place. For a region to be without a church means that it does not have the access it needs to the truth of God's goodness and love. Lacking a church is not equivalent to lacking a decent supermarket or movie theatre; it is like lacking a hospital or a source of water. It is an utter necessity.

We see this priority reflected throughout the New Testament. The world needs a church, in every place. Think about Paul's instruction to his younger colleague, Titus:

> The reason I left you in Crete was that you might put in order what was left unfinished and appoint elders in every town, as I directed you.   *Titus 1 v 5*

Notice Paul does not say "elders in every church". Churches need leadership (as we'll see in due course). But Paul's point is broader. It is not just the case that every church needs a leader, but that every town needs a church. Paul's concern is with mission. For the gospel to penetrate the urban centres of Crete, there needs to be at least one church in every town. Churches are God's way to reach whole regions.

We see this in Paul's own mission activity. When he spends time in a given city, he does not just seek to make a few disciples here and there, and then considers his job to be done. He forms an assembly—a church—and appoints elders to oversee and lead them. He is not just wanting converts, but churches.

The world did not need my old tennis club. And it did not need me to be committed to that tennis club (they seem to have managed quite well without me). But the world does need the church. My local area needs the local church I'm part of. Your local area needs your church too. Church is foundational and central to what God is doing in his world.

The church is the bride of Jesus

In one of the final passages in the Bible, the elderly apostle John is given a glimpse of the future, of the day when God recreates the cosmos for his people to enjoy in perfection, for ever. It's an amazing vision; and one of the most amazing aspects is how the church—what Revelation calls "the new Jerusalem"—is described, and dressed:

> I saw "a new heaven and a new earth," for the first heaven and the first earth had passed away, and there was no longer any sea. I saw the Holy City, the new Jerusalem, coming down out of heaven from God, prepared as a bride beautifully dressed for her husband.   *Revelation 21 v 1-2*

The church is a bride—a beautiful one. Whose bride? John already knows:

> The wedding of the Lamb has come, and his bride has made herself ready. Fine linen, bright and clean, was given her to wear. (Fine linen stands for the righteous acts of God's holy people.)
> *19 v 7-8*

The church is the beautiful bride of the Lamb—of Jesus himself. And so the day of Jesus' return will be a wedding feast—and Christians are invited to it not as guests, but as the bride. None of us will have to sneak into heaven through the back door—we'll be walking up the aisle.

All this seems strange to us, because the marriage we're used to is not between the Son of God and his church, but between two people. But actually, the human marriages that happen all the time are pictures of this greater one (Ephesians 5 v 22-33)—this is the ultimate relationship, the only marriage that endures for eternity.

If you want to understand how committed Jesus is to the church, here's your answer. He doesn't just create it and let it be. He marries it. He is not just our almighty King; he is also our perfect Husband. That's how much concern he has for every member of his church. That's how much he cares about local church. That's how committed he is to us, for ever.

This is even more amazing when we appreciate who the church is. At the end of time, at the wedding feast of the Lamb, the church will look beautiful, but only because clean, righteous "linen" will be "given her to wear" (Revelation 19 v 8). This promise of what the church will be in the future is a wonderful assurance that one day she will be perfect. But it is also a reminder that she is sadly still very imperfect in this present age. She is not yet the beauty she will one day be. Alongside the wonderful status we have as God's people there is still considerable ugliness and failure. We are not yet the bride we should be.

In the Old Testament, God had used a human marriage to show what his people were like. He told one of his prophets, Hosea, to...

Go, marry a promiscuous woman and have children with her, for like an adulterous wife this land [that is, God's people, living in Israel] is guilty of unfaithfulness to the LORD. *Hosea 1 v 2*

Hosea's wife was adulterous—she cheated on her husband. And God is saying that his people were, and are, spiritually adulterous. That's what sin is—it is loving something more than God; it is cheating on God. Spiritually speaking, the church is unfaithful.

Yet Jesus is the Husband of the church. And as Hosea was sent to "Go, show your love to your wife again, though she is loved by another man and is an adulteress" (3 v 1), Jesus still loves us, despite what we're like. And as Hosea had to pay "fifteen shekels of silver and about a homer and a lethek of barley" (v 2) to free his wife to live with him again—a high price—so Jesus paid his own life to free us to live with him for ever—the highest price. That's how much he loves his church. All we bring to this relationship is our need and our guilt. But he brings freedom, a "dress" worth wearing, and a perfect future with him for ever.

So the church is the beloved bride of Jesus. Church is not his hobby; it is his marriage—and it's ours too. Think about what it means to be church in this way and it becomes exciting, and all the more so when we recognise what we're like as his people. We will gather on a Sunday, look round and look at ourselves, and be absolutely amazed at who we are before him. We will hear about who he is in his word, and sing about who he is in our hymns, and be completely awestruck that we get to be part of his bride. And we will live each day safe and secure in the knowledge that Jesus could not care more about his church: he died for it.

Hasn't the church done more harm than good?

"The church" has not had a flawless track record. We can think of sexual abuse scandals that have racked a number of prominent denominations. We can think of the medieval Crusades, the Inquisition of the 1500s and 1600s, or the 20th-century Troubles in Northern Ireland. And we can think of hypocrisy and judgmentalism, which has hit the headlines time and time again. Looking at all this, some might suppose the church is more trouble than it's worth.

As Christians, it is very important that we acknowledge the times when Christians have done wrong in the name of Christ, as well as remembering that we need to distinguish between those who were truly Christians and gravely mistaken and those who claimed to be Christians, acted in the name of "the church", but in fact were not living with Christ as their King and Saviour and did not seek to live by what he says in the Bible. We must not deny that such things have happened. There have been many occasions in which Christians have not honoured the name of their Lord. Trying to whitewash this will not help at all.

But as we are honest about these failings, it is helpful to remember some key gospel truths. Both common grace and sin are universal. By common grace, we mean the fact that though everyone is a sinner, no one is as sinful as they could be, all the time: God has restrained us. We are still capable of being caring friends and productive workers, all the while being in rebellion against God. And at the same time, giving up our rebellion against God and coming under his rule—

joining his church—does not mean we cease to be sinful. None of us will be perfect until the day we stand before Christ when he returns.

This means that there will always be instances of human goodness outside the church, and instances of sin within it. Our concern is not to try to prove that every Christian is always better than every non-Christian. It is inevitable that no Christian lives out the gospel with complete consistency. We should not settle for that, but we do need to admit that.

We also need to remember that the Bible frequently and powerfully critiques the sins of hypocrisy and self-righteousness. The Old Testament prophets spent far more time condemning the sins of God's people than those of the nations around them. Jesus' own strongest condemnations were against the religious, not the irreligious. Inevitable though Christian inconsistency may be, we are never to make peace with it. When Christians are being violent and judgmental, they are being so not in obedience to Jesus, but in defiance of what he taught us.

Alongside the failings of Christians and churches have been many instances where the gospel has been truly reflected. Yes, the church has been guilty of wrong. It is most likely far worse than we've realised, because not every failing reaches the light of day. But if the church has been far worse than we might think, it has also been far better too. It was Christians—Bible-believing people—who spearheaded the movement to abolish slavery. It was early Christians who bought slaves in order to set them free. It was Christians who were at the heart of the civil rights movement in the USA, and Christians who led the reconciliation movement in post-apartheid South Africa. Today, a huge amount of charitable and relief work takes place throughout the world through Christian agencies, often unreported and unnoticed.

The church has done harm, because the church is made up of sinful people. But that is not the whole story, because the church is made up of saved people who are being made more and more like Jesus. And, at the end of the day, it is not the church we preach, but Christ. It is his life, death and resurrection—not our track record—that we take our stand on, and that we strive to point people to, both with our words and with our deeds.

Chapter 2

Why do I need church?

t is a conversation I've had countless times over the years. It might be with the hairdresser, or the person next to me on the train, or someone I meet at a party. We start chatting, it comes up that I'm a pastor, and they talk warmly about Christianity before adding something along the lines of:

> *"I follow Jesus, but I don't do church. I don't have anything against it—I just don't need it. I'm fine on my own."*

Can't I be a Christian without church?

Throughout the Bible, we see that God's plan is to make a people for himself. This is crucial. God's purpose is not to have persons relating to him individually, but a people that, together, are his. God's promise to Abraham was that he would be the father of "a great nation" (Genesis 12 v 2). The vision of heaven that the apostle John is given right at the end of the Bible is of a "great multitude that no one could count" worshipping God together (Revelation 7 v 9). God has always promised there would be a people for himself.

This means that part of God's work in drawing people to himself is drawing his people to one another. When he saves, he gathers. Individuals who come to Christ are assembled together with one another.

One of the features of Western culture today is individualism. Back in the 17th century, when the philosopher René Descartes attempted to begin a defence for God with the words, "I think, therefore I am", he kicked off something of a trend: starting the answer to life's questions with "I". Nowadays we tend to think that the basic unit of all reality is me. Everything else is defined in relation to me.

Technology has accelerated this trend. Our entertainment, communication, books, hobbies, finance, work and lifestyle are more and more personalised. A previous generation would have gathered to watch TV. The generation before that would have gathered to listen to the radio. Now we can do either on our own pretty much anywhere.

None of this makes such technology a bad thing, of course (I'm writing this on a laptop, drawing on notes filed on my smartphone, all in a very individualised way). But there is a great danger that we end up approaching the Christian life with a similar mindset. After all, we can get regular podcasts of the best Bible teaching out there. We can download the latest and best worship music. We can pray wherever we are. I can have "church" while lying in bed on a Sunday morning. Why bother getting up and hauling myself down the road to a church where neither the teaching nor music will be as good? Can't I just have Jesus? Does Christianity have to come with Christians?

The New Testament challenges this instinct with two huge and unmissable truths.

1. You can't come to Christ without coming to his people

Paul shows us how our relationship with Christ shapes our relationship with one another:

> In Christ Jesus you are all children of God through faith, for all of you who were baptised into Christ have clothed yourselves with Christ. There is nei-ther Jew nor Gentile, neither slave nor free, nor is there male and female, for you are all one in Christ Jesus. *Galatians 3 v 26-28*

As Christians we are united to Christ—we are baptised into him and clothed with him (meaning he gives us his perfect record, and changes us to become more and more like him). And being united to Jesus means we are united to everyone else who is united to Jesus. We are "all one in Christ Jesus".

This is true of the whole worldwide, universal church. Through faith in Christ, we are one with Christians around the world we may never even meet. Wherever we are in the world, we are not far from family. But it's in the local church that this oneness is to be particularly expressed and worked out.

Paul likens the church to a human body:

> In Christ we, though many, form one body, and each member belongs to all the others.
>
> *Romans 12 v 5*

Notice the implication: being formed together into one body gives us an obligation. We belong to the rest of the body. It is impossible to be in Christ and not belong to others. A Christian, by definition, has a connection with and a responsibility to other Christians. You cannot claim Christ and avoid his people. If God is your Father, then his people are your family, and you are to treat your family as your Father wants you to.

Church is therefore not a meeting you attend, but a body you belong to.

Elsewhere, Paul builds on this idea and describes the church as "the body of Christ" (1 Corinthians 12 v 27). This is an insight that was burned onto Paul's consciousness from his very first encounter with the risen Christ. When Jesus appeared to him, Paul (then known as "Saul") had been aggressively and systematically trying to stamp out Christianity. Jesus's words to him were stunning and life-changing: "Why do you persecute me? ... I am Jesus, whom you are persecuting" (Acts 9 v 4-5). Twice, Jesus accuses Paul of persecuting him. The implication was clear: by persecuting the church, Paul was persecuting Jesus. The relationship between Jesus and his people is so tight that what you do to them, you do to him.

This insight never left Paul, and it should never leave us. Christ utterly identifies with his people.

2. You can't serve Christ without serving his people.

What you do to the church, you do to Jesus. And when you fail to serve the church, you fail to serve Jesus. We see this in the teaching of Jesus himself:

> Truly I tell you, whatever you did for one of the least of these brothers and sisters of mine, you did for me. *Matthew 25 v 40*

Jesus is not talking about serving people in general, but about his "brothers and sisters"—his people. The New Testament has much to say about helping the needy in general, but it is when it comes to his own people that Jesus tells us that what is done for them is done for him. Again, how we treat his people is how we treat him. If we serve our (and his!) brothers and sisters, we serve him. The reverse is also true. If we fail to serve his people, we fail to serve him. Neglecting the church is neglecting Jesus. Doing "church" in my bedroom on my own isn't starting to look so good...

There will be unavoidable reasons why some Christians are unable to come to church for a while. There are those who are physically frail, or recovering from a psychological trauma that makes time with crowds especially difficult. There might be family circumstances or emergencies that call us away for a while. But these must be exceptions. If you harden your heart to the needs of God's people around you, you are effectively closing your heart to Christ.

But the reverse is also and wonderfully true: when you do take God's people seriously and commit to them, when you are of service, Jesus says that "whatever you did for one of the least of these brothers and sisters of mine, you did for me."

So what do I miss out on if I don't join a church?

The biblical answer to this is "Heaps".

Church, as we've seen, is the local gathering of God's people. It's not the denomination, and its not the building. But neither is it just the teaching and music, because it is possible to experience those things without actually being around other Christians. The point of preaching and worship is that they are corporate activities. And therein lies the heart of what a church-skipping believer misses out on: God's people.

The attempt to have Jesus without the church is evidently not new. The writer to the Hebrews says that people were trying it in his day too:

Let us consider how we may spur one another on towards love and good deeds, not giving up meeting together, as some are in the habit of doing, but encouraging one another—and all the more as you see the Day approaching.

Hebrews 10 v 24-25

Some were already in the habit of not meeting together. This is not a modern tendency. People were trying to ditch church 2,000 years ago too.

But notice what the alternative is: "Not giving up meeting together ... but encouraging one another". One church I know decided to use these verses as a motto on all their church literature. But a clumsy oversight on the part of the printer meant that the leaflets all came back without the word "not", so that the end result actually commended readers to consider giving up meeting together! But the point of the passage is clear. One of the reasons church is vital is that the practice of meeting together is one of the key ways in which God encourages us in our faith. We have been designed to need other Christians to help us keep going in the faith, and to whom we can be an encouragement to do likewise.

The urgency of this mutual encouragement is spelt out in the final words of these verses: "All the more as you see the Day approaching".

As I write, signs have started to appear in shop windows and all over the media, alerting me to a day that is coming, and telling me that I must prepare for it: Christmas. Annoyingly, it's still only August—it seems a little premature. But the point is a sound one: the Christmas holidays are something that will come, and that need to be prepared for.

But the writer to the Hebrews reminds us that there is another day approaching, infinitely more significant than the holidays—the return of Jesus Christ. And the way to prepare for that day is to be encouraged in our faith in Christ, and to be growing in love and good deeds that flow from this faith. To do that we need the input of others, and to have input into others. That is how God has designed his people to flourish. Outside of the local church, we will lack the encouragement God has for us, and we will be failing to help others grow in their faith too. To think we will carry on our Christian lives is therefore a little arrogant—I'm saying I can manage without the encouragement that God wants to provide me with through the local church—and quite selfish—I'm saying that I won't encourage those in my local church.

This encouragement will take a variety of forms. The New Testament talks of us "building one another up" in the faith, and of times when we need carefully to correct and sometimes even rebuke one another (1 Thessalonians 5 v 11; 2 Thessalonians 3 v 15; Galatians 6 v 1). Church will be where we find inspiration. I think of an elderly sister in Christ, increasingly frail and in pain, and yet who is a constant reminder of what a comfort it is to walk with Jesus. I think of a wise brother who, often with just an aside, reminds me of the joy we have in knowing our sin is forgiven. There are countless more examples: people who have persevered through horrific suffering or who pour themselves into the lives of others. People, in short, who in any number of ways remind me that Christ is worth it.

The church is where there will be a loving challenge and accountability—where our Christian profession is properly examined to see if it is genuine. It is the church that can welcome new members through baptism, and encourage the faithful through sharing of the Lord's

Supper. In all these ways we are spurred on in our faith. Without the church we lose vital spiritual momentum.

But failure to be involved in a local church means we miss out on more than spiritual encouragement:

> By this everyone will know that you are my disciples, if you love one another. *John 13 v 35*

A significant part of the church's evangelistic impact will be due to the quality of relationships it demonstrates between its members. Jesus says it is the defining mark of true discipleship: we most show ourselves to be his followers when we exhibit his self-giving love to other disciples. Jesus assumes that the quality of relationships between his followers will be of a kind found nowhere else.

And it will not just be other disciples who recognise the supernatural origins of this love, but "everyone". The world will not be able to attribute this love to anything other than the presence of Jesus in the lives of these people.

In other words, the life of God's people together will have a huge impact on the world around us. It is in this context—the corporate life of the church—that we learn how to live out the love that Christ has shown us. It is here we sharpen our sense of what it means to be disciples, and become trained up in distinctive sacrificial love. Jesus' expectation is that the kind of love we have for one another will be found nowhere else on earth.

This means that to not be part of the church is to miss out on one of the most powerful evangelistic tools God has given us. It is in the life of the church that gospel truth is lived out and worked through in practice. Mark Dever captures this in the title of his excellent book, *The Church: The Gospel Made Visible*. The gospel truths we seek to share with others become literally fleshed out when they come along to a genuine Christian church.

Needy, and needed

We've already seen that, more than once, Paul describes the church as a body. And in 1 Corinthians 12, he draws some very simple, but key, implications. Paul writes:

> If the foot should say, "Because I am not a hand, I do not belong to the body," it would not for that reason stop being part of the body. *v 15*

Your church needs you. You may not have the gifts you wish you had, or that seem the most important or visible, but you are as vital to the health of the church as anyone else. There will be a contribution you can make to your church that is unique to you.

Here's an exercise for you. Take a pen, a piece of paper and a timer. How many times can you write your name in 30 seconds? Now try the same exercise but without using your hands. You can put the pen between your toes or hold it in your mouth. My guess is, you didn't do so well the second time round. Once you remove certain parts of the body, even simple tasks get harder. It reminds us of how much those with disability deserve our admiration. And it also reminds us of what our church misses out on when we are not there—part of the body is missing. Your church needs you.

And you need your church:

> The eye cannot say to the hand, "I don't need you!" ... On the contrary, those parts of the body that seem to be weaker are indispensable. *v 21-22*

Whether you're the preacher or a child, whether you've been a Christian for four weeks or four decades, whether you're the most successful businessperson or the longest-term unemployed, you need everyone else as much as they need you.

The truth is that "God has placed the parts in the body, every one of them, just as he wanted them to be ... there are many parts, but one body" (v 18, 20). The membership of every local church is no accident; it is by divine design. There is no one there who is a spare part, a third foot or second nose. There is no one there who is not necessary, or who doesn't need the rest of their church. That includes you—which is really quite exciting. God has chosen to include and to use you. You can make a real, lasting, eternally significant difference by being a part of your church. Your church is vital to you, and you are vital to your church.

Chapter 3

What makes a good church?

What should a church actually *do*? Ask ten members of a church congregation that question, and you'll probably get ten (or maybe more!) answers. There are almost an infinite number of good things that a church should be doing—and, because churches contain as many imperfect people as they contain members, there'll always be some sense that a church is not doing what it could, or should.

A growing church has to ask difficult questions about what its priorities should be. A dwindling church has to ask those same questions, but they will be asked with more frustration or anxiety. A static church ought to be asking the very same questions. What do God's people, gathered by him in a particular place, spend their time and give their energies to doing?

In Acts 2, Luke gives us a picture of the early Christian church. Jesus had only recently ascended into heaven and, just as he promised, the Holy Spirit had come to empower his people. The impact was dramatic. Peter had just preached and more than 3,000 people had joined the Christian community. And next, we're given a snapshot of the church life that developed among these believers, and it shows us the marks of a Spirit-filled church. Take a moment to read Acts 2 v 42-47.

1. Learning

This is the first thing Luke shows us about the church:

> They devoted themselves to the apostles' teaching.
>
> *v 42*

This is to be the mark of all believers. "Disciple" means "learner", and so all who come to Christ begin a lifelong process of learning more from him and about him. The apostles were the group specially authorised by Jesus to pass on his word to the early church. They had all met with the risen Jesus and had been appointed to speak for him, and so their teaching had and has a unique authority for Christians. This authority is reflected in what Luke goes on to say about them:

> Everyone was filled with awe at the many wonders and signs performed by the apostles. *v 43*

This was one of the ways in which their unique authority was accredited. It doesn't mean miracles have never been performed by anybody else since, but the amount of miracles we see going on through the apostles is one of the things that marked them out as apostles (see 2 Corinthians 12 v 12), just as Jesus' miracles pointed towards his identity as the Son of God (John 2 v 11). Such miraculous acts served to underline the way in which their teaching bore the authority of Jesus himself.

It is this teaching that has been recorded and preserved for us in the pages of the New Testament. We don't need to worry about the fact that we weren't there to hear the apostles for ourselves; we have our Bibles. A sign that the Holy Spirit is at work among us is that we are devoted to the teaching of the apostles in the Bible.

A key priority for any church, therefore, is to spend time learning from the Bible together. Our preaching needs to be based on it, and our songs, hymns and prayers need to reflect it. Those who lead us need to be skilled in unpacking this teaching for us, laying it out before us in a way that is easy to grasp and apply. We need to give adequate time to the teaching of God's word in our meetings, and make sure other things do not squeeze it out.

And we need, as individual Christians, to come to our church gatherings expecting to learn from the Bible, and excited about doing so. Luke does not tell us that the apostles were devoted to teaching—that was necessary, but not sufficient. He tells us that the Christians were devoted to listening to their teaching. (People sometimes say that my church is known for having "good teaching". I would far rather it was known for having great learning!) If we know what passage of Scripture is being preached on at church, it will help to read and think about it during the week beforehand, asking ourselves what God might have for us in this part of his word. We should pray for the pastor as he prepares to preach, and for ourselves as we prepare to hear, that God might ready us for what he will say to us. In some churches it might be possible to ask questions about the sermon, or to discuss the passage in small groups later that week. However we might express it, we need to be devoted to learning from God's word.

2. Partnership

> They devoted themselves to the apostles' teaching and to fellowship, to the breaking of bread and to prayer. *Acts 2 v 42*

This church's commitment to learning is followed by their commitment to one another. This sequence should not surprise us, for it is the very teaching of the apostles that reminds us of all that binds us together as fellow believers in Christ. One of the signs that a church is drifting from the apostolic gospel is that its fellowship is becoming more and more superficial.

It's easy for us to misunderstand the word "fellowship" and to assume it is the mysterious condition that appears whenever two Christians encounter one another in the presence of coffee. But the word for fellowship in the New Testament—*koinonia*—can just as easily be translated as "partnership". It is the word you would use to describe two colleagues who have gone into business together. To be committed to fellowship is to be conscious of how you are now partners in the same venture.

It speaks of our common goal and of how we have a stake in one another as Christians.

We see this partnership in the early church in a couple of key ways. First of all, they shared their time. They hung out together a lot:

> All the believers were together ... Every day they continued to meet together in the temple courts. They broke bread in their homes and ate together with glad and sincere hearts. *v 44, 46*

We need to bear in mind that it was still Pentecost at this point, their equivalent of the school holidays, and so it might not be that they carried on meeting daily after this time—we're not told. But it does show that their reflex as fellow-believers was to spend time with one another. The attitude was more "How much time can we spend together?" than "How much time must we spend together?"

Luke particularly draws attention to how often they ate together, twice mentioning that they regularly broke bread (v 42 and v 46). And as they broke bread and shared meals together, they would no doubt have shared in the Lord's Supper at the same time (see 1 Corinthians 11 v 17-34). The bread and the wine would have been shared in the context of a whole meal together. It is a reminder that church members are to share their lives with one another.

"Fellowship" is not just twenty minutes after church on a Sunday until the cookies have run out or the Sunday lunch needs getting out of the oven. Some of us find that easier than others. Some of us love being in a crowded room; others dread it. That's OK! We are all wired differently. We don't have to be someone we're not (as we've seen, the church being a body made up of varying parts means the church actually needs us to be the person we are). But equally, we do need to be people who work hard at this and who are willing to step out of our comfort zones to spend time together. For an extrovert, that may mean learning to listen well. For an introvert, that may mean diving into conversations we don't feel we have the energy for. Fellowship is hard work, but it is worth it.

Then second, in addition to sharing their time, they also shared their possessions. These Christians had "everything in common" (Acts 2 v 44). That's not to say none of them were allowed anything of their own. Luke speaks in the same passage of people having homes and possessions. What we see here is not forced collectivism, but radical generosity. The members of this church were eager to share what they had in order to meet any needs that arose among them. And it's clear that this goes far beyond selling off little trinkets here and there. People were willing to sell their land for the sake of others (Acts 4 v 36-37)—in today's terms, that's the equivalent of giving up your life savings.

In my experience of working in a couple of churches, it has been wonderful to see many instances of this sort of thing happening frequently. I've seen church members pay for a family to go on a holiday they wouldn't otherwise have been able to afford; people loaning or donating cars to one another; accommodation being provided for minimal and sometimes even no rent.

There are countless examples of lifts and meals being provided for those in need.

But it would be foolish to think that material generosity is not still a huge challenge for many of our churches today. Many of us live in cultures that prize the accumulation of material possessions more than pretty much anything else, and we'd be naïve to think it is not a weakness for us in the church as well. We need to work on our attitude to our possessions, seeing all that we have as gifts from God to be used for his purposes by being shared with his people. We need to hold lightly to the things we own and the money we have and the places where we live.

3. Worship

This church enjoyed making much of God.

They were devoted to prayer (2 v 42). It was a feature of these Christians that their time together was marked by prayer. In the chapters that follow, we see them praying in response to persecution, and praying when they needed guidance. When Peter is arrested and thrown in prison, they all pile round to one of their homes to pray—even in the middle of the night. Praying wasn't something this community of believers did out of duty or obligation. It was no hardship and no chore. That is the mark of a church touched by the Holy Spirit!

For many of us, church prayer meetings may not be easy. Perhaps they are not well led, or lack variety. Certainly, praying with others, out loud, is hard work. But, as we've seen with other aspects of church life, what is hard work is often what is vital work. We need to pray with our church family.

We also see their worship in their praise of God:

> They broke bread in their homes and ate together with glad and sincere hearts, praising God. *v 46-47*

To praise someone or something is to speak well of them or it. It comes naturally whenever we come across something that delights us. We'll instinctively go on about a great movie we've seen, or something great our kids have done for us. We praise all sorts of things. And supremely, this church praised God, in a joyful (glad), wholehearted (sincere) way. Joy in God seemed to mark their corporate life, whatever they were doing together. They knew their God to be unfathomably good and enjoyed reflecting that in the way they spent time with one another.

This praise would have included singing, as other places in the New Testament make clear (for instance, Ephesians 5 v 19-20; Colossians 3 v 16). God's people have always been singers, because God has always given his people good cause to sing. Joyful praise will mark any healthy church.

It does us good to rehearse in song all that God is and has done for his people. Singing is, first, a great way of encouraging one another—if you realise a hymn or song is addressed to others, rather than God, why not look at those around you as you sing it (it seems weird at first, but gets more normal!) And second, it is also a wonderful way to encourage ourselves, internalising gospel truth and declaring it afresh to our souls. Many of us can remember song lyrics far more easily than we can Bible verses or the main points of last Sunday's sermon (let alone from the Sunday before)—so it's wise to make sure the songs we hum on a Wednesday morning or a Saturday afternoon are ones that focus on the gospel.

4. Growth

The early Christian church saw enormous growth:

> And the Lord added to their number daily those who were being saved. *Acts 2 v 47*

Luke reminds us that it is God who does the growing. It was not these Christians who converted people; God added to their number. Any growth—in number or in maturity—is God's work, not ours. It is interesting that Luke doesn't mention evangelism in this snapshot. We know that these Christians were active in sharing their faith (the chapters of Acts that follow make that abundantly clear), but it is God who gives the growth.

I suspect Luke's point is that any church like the one he has described will grow. Devotion to the teaching of the apostles, tangible partnership with one another, and heartfelt praise and worship of God together will produce a community deeply compelling to a watching world. It is a church God will tend to grow!

But such a church will also have a hunger to grow. We cannot enjoy the gospel without being burdened for the lost. The message of Jesus is the best news we can ever hear, and we have a responsibility to share that message with all who've not heard it.

The early church, it seems, didn't need to be told to do evangelism. They simply did it. The gospel contains its own evangelistic impetus. Peter, whose evangelistic talk God used to bring this first church into being and who was one of its first leaders, would later tell the churches of what is now modern-day Turkey that they existed to "declare the praises of him who called you out of darkness into his wonderful light"; that they must "live such good lives among the pagans that ... they may see your good deeds and glorify God on the day he visits us"; and that they should "always be prepared to give an answer to everyone who asks you to give the reason for the hope that you have ... with gentleness and respect" (1 Peter 2 v 9, 12; 3 v 15).

A healthy church will be thinking about how they can declare God's praise to their community, in both their gathered meetings and when their members are scattered throughout that community during the week. They will exhort each other to live in a way that reflects the beauty of the gospel, and equip each other so that they are ready to speak the truth of the gospel to those who ask them the big questions of life.

This concern for the wider community is not just limited to evangelism. The people of God today, as in the Old Testament, are to "seek the peace and prosperity" of the cities in which they find themselves (Jeremiah 29 v 7). Paul tells us to "do good to all people, especially to those who belong to the family of believers" (Galatians 6 v 10). Notice that he says "especially", not "primarily", and certainly not "only". Charity does begin at home, but it does not end there.

Churches are both to declare and display the gospel in how they treat each other, and in how they treat those who live around them.

Priorities

All churches are different. They hold their services at different times; their styles of worship together are different; their sizes are very different. But all Christian churches will have these priorities in common—and these will (or should be) priorities not only for those tasked with leading the church, but for "all the believers" (Acts 2 v 44), whom Christ purchased with his blood:

- Apostolic teaching
- Partnership
- Worship
- Growth

This makes being church and doing church both very simple, and very hard. Simple, because these things are not difficult to understand. Hard, because it's far easier to join a tennis club or go to a park—something we can dip in and out of, according to our mood and circumstances—than it is to be a biblical church. Easier, but less exciting. I don't imagine these early Christians always found being part of this church convenient, and it was rarely cost-free (especially once persecution started). But I don't imagine they found it dull or dutiful either; and I imagine it must have been thrilling to watch the Lord at work in and through them as he "added to their number daily those who were being saved" (v 47). And if we would love to experience what that church experienced, we need to commit to being, and pray about becoming, a church like that one, with the same priorities.

How should I pick a church?

1. *Plan ahead.* Before moving anywhere (assuming you have a choice in the matter), be sure there will be a good church to join. It is foolish to go somewhere where there will not be good spiritual support and leadership. So do all you can to investigate this before making a decision to move there. Places which seem spiritually barren do, of course, need Christians to move there in order for there to be the potential for a good church to begin. But there is a huge difference between Christians being commissioned and sent to an area to plant a new church, and those who end up in such an area without giving local-church involvement any serious thought in advance. I can think of many people who have moved to a new area because of a dream job, or because they always wanted to retire to the coast, and who found themselves without a good church and spiritually stagnating for years as a result.

2. *Be discerning.* We have already seen the marks of a good church. These matter, and should shape what you look for in a church more than anything else. Whether Christ is truly preached, followed, shared and loved matters far more than whether a church has your kind of coffee, meets at your preferred time of day, or is super-convenient to get to.

3. *Don't take too long.* If you move to an area with lots of possible good churches to go to, there is a danger of taking too long over deciding which to

join. It can become like channel-hopping on TV, where we take so much time seeing what is on that we end up spending an hour or two without actually watching anything. Church-hoppers do the rounds of all the possible churches, never really settling, and before they know it, a year has passed and they've still not joined a church.

Where we find ourselves with seemingly bountiful choice, it can be good to set ourselves a time limit—two or three months, perhaps—for making a final decision. Checking out churches in advance via their websites means we can make a shortlist before we've even moved there.

4. *Don't be too quick.* It can be tempting to join the first good church you find. But finding the right church to join is worth taking some time, thought and prayer over. You really want to be sure this is a church family that will grow you in Christ and encourage you to serve others.

Remember that a single visit to a church may not be truly representative. Those of us who work for churches know that there are plenty of "off Sundays" where everything seems to go wrong: the sermon is muddled, the AV system is on the blink, people who are meant to have turned up to do something have forgotten, and the whole thing is—humanly speaking—a bit of a shambles. These things happen. We live in a fallen world. Give any church the benefit of the doubt, make sure you are looking for positives as well as noticing less-good aspects, and make an effort to visit a church more than once, particularly if everything else you know about them suggests they are a healthy church to belong to.

What are baptism and communion for?

These are two particular ceremonies that Jesus has commanded his church to perform—in some churches they are called "ordinances", in others "sacraments", and in others neither! Both are hugely important (otherwise Jesus would not have commanded them) and both have become issues over which Bible-believing Christians have had differing views over the years. It might be helpful to think of baptism as the "front door" of the church, and communion as "the family meal". The first is to do with initiation into the church; the second with ongoing membership of it.

Baptism: Jesus commands his disciples to be baptised: "Go and make disciples of all nations, baptising them in the name of the Father and of the Son and of the Holy Spirit, and teaching them to obey everything I have commanded you" (Matthew 28 v 19-20). Baptism is not necessary for salvation, but it is necessary for obedience. Disciples are to be baptised.

The act of baptism itself speaks of receiving a new birth, being washed (Titus 3 v 5), and of being united to Christ (Romans 6 v 3-4). We have been baptised into Jesus. Our old self has died with him and our new self has been raised with him (Galatians 2 v 20). Bible-believing Christians differ over the mode of baptism (whether someone should be fully immersed in water or sprinkled) and over when it is appropriate for someone to be baptised (whether as an infant in a Christian family or as a professing adult). If you want to think about these questions in more detail, the best way to do so is to speak to your pastor.

Communion: Different churches call this different names. The most common are Holy Communion (emphasising our fellowship with God), the Lord's Supper (emphasising that this is a meal at which Jesus is head), or the Eucharist (which means "thanksgiving").

Communion is a moment, in the gathered worship of the church, when Christians share bread and wine together. This may be bread from a physical loaf distributed among the congregation, or individual portions cut before the service, or dry wafer-like pieces. Some churches will use alcoholic wine, others non-alcoholic wine—some will have both. It might be served in a chalice shared among the congregation or distributed in small individual cups. Churches might celebrate it every week, every month, or less frequently.

Though the practice will therefore vary, the purpose of communion is clear. It is a way of remembering the broken body and shed blood of Jesus (1 Corinthians 11 v 24-25); of proclaiming that death (11 v 26); of having fellowship with Christ (10 v 16); and of expressing our common dependence on Jesus as a group of believers (10 v 17). It is a wonderful, evocative meal that the Lord has given to us and invited us to share! So it is not to be taken lightly. Paul calls us to examine ourselves before we receive it (11 v 28). We need to make sure we are in appropriate good relational standing both with God and with his people. But equally, in the New Testament communion is not central to the life of the church, nor essential for salvation (it is not mentioned in the three letters Paul wrote to pastors—1 and 2 Timothy and Titus). As the theologian Ernest Kevan once put it, "Communion is a special means of grace, not a means of special grace".

Chapter 4

How is church run?

Some time ago I was leafing through the pages of a denominational newspaper, and came across adverts churches had placed for new pastors. It was fascinating to see what all these churches were looking for in a leader.

Successful candidates needed to be able administrators (which rules me out) and visionary leaders (ditto). One stipulated that its pastor must be "highly visible within the church" (which rules me in—I have a high-viz jacket I could use). Other adverts were looking for exceptional counsellors, community workers and entrepreneurs. The adverts all seemed to have their own very distinct idea about what a pastor is meant to do.

But, for all their variety, they did agree on one thing: their church did need to be led.

This need for leadership is very clear throughout Scripture. The people of God are not just led by God himself, but they experience his leading through properly appointed human leaders. What this looks like may vary from church to church (as we'll see), but it is very clear that there is always some form of human leadership.

This chapter is about "church government" or "church polity". Depending on which church you're part of, this chapter will either be shorter and less detailed, or longer and more detailed, than you are used to or would like. How our churches should be led has become an issue over which there has been considerable discussion over the years. Of course, there is room for legitimate disagreement between Christians on this issue. But we need to remember to be generous to those who think differently on, or simply less of, this issue than we do. We also need to remember that we are saved through faith in Jesus, not because we belong to a church with or without bishops, or presbyteries, or a congregational model (or because we do or don't know what the difference between all of that is!).

Elders and deacons

The most common word in the New Testament to describe such leaders is "elders". We see this in a number of places. When Paul planted churches, he was sure to appoint elders to lead them before himself moving on to plant elsewhere. It was not enough for him to see a group of Christians established in a particular place; there needed to be appropriate leadership put in place for them. In Acts, for example, we're told:

> Paul and Barnabas appointed elders for them in
> each church and, with prayer and fasting, com-
> mitted them to the Lord. *Acts 14 v 23*

The work of properly setting up a church was not finished until this step had been taken.

An important feature of this leadership is that it is
always plural. The New Testament never speaks of a
church having just one leader, but instead describes a
number of elders being appointed. It is the plural elders
from the church in Ephesus that Paul called to a meeting (Acts 20 v 17), and who laid their hands on Timothy
at the formal start of his ministry there (1 Timothy 4
v 14). Nowhere does the New Testament envisage a ministry equivalent of a one-man band, where there will
be no one able to offer vital challenge or support. The
church needs leadership, and no one individual leader
will be sufficient for this. Elders are always plural.

Other terminology besides "elders" is used to describe church leaders. Paul refers to them as "pastors"
(Ephesians 4 v 11). Elsewhere they are described as
"overseers" or "bishops" (translating the Greek word
episkopos, from which we get the word "episcopal").
Though these are two different terms, it is clear that
both describe the same office. Paul says to the elders in
Ephesus, "Keep watch over yourselves and all the flock
of which the Holy Spirit has made you overseers" (Acts
20 v 28). "Overseer/bishop" here simply highlights an
aspect of what it means to be an elder; it is not itself a
whole separate office (even though it has come to be so
in some denominations).

As well as the role of elders, the New Testament also describes the role of deacons within the running of the local church. This is distinct from the role of an elder. As he introduces his letter to the Philippians, Paul writes, "To all God's holy people in Christ Jesus at Philippi, together with the overseers and deacons" (Philippians 1 v 1). This is a separate role to that of an elder/overseer, and seems to be focused more on practical and administrative duties. In the early church, deacons were appointed specifically so that the apostles could be free to focus on the ministry of God's word (Acts 6 v 1-6). Although their role is never fully spelled out in the New Testament, deacons appear to have been appointed to serve the church in a variety of ways. Unlike elders they do not have ruling authority, but as with elders, Paul lists specific qualifications for this role (1 Timothy 3 v 8-13).

What should church leadership look like?

These principles of how churches are run map onto different churches today in a variety of ways. There are **four** main ways that church leadership tends to be structured today. Most churches will fall into one of these.

1. Episcopalian. This is where local churches together form part of a diocese overseen by a bishop, who is himself overseen by an archbishop. Each bishop therefore oversees a number of congregations, and each archbishop oversees a number of bishops. The local congregation itself will have its own pastor (often called a rector or a vicar), as well as office-holders such as church wardens and a parochial church council. Under this system, a certain amount of authority lies outside the local congregation. The Church of England and the Anglican Church of North America are examples of episcopalian denominations. Although (as we've seen) the New Testament does not use the word "bishop" to describe a separate office in this way, episcopalians would see the role of bishops in their denomination as a continuation of the wider roles of men like Titus in the New Testament.

2. Presbyterian. "Presbyterian" comes from the Greek word for elder, and indicates that it is the elders who are the focus of decision-making authority in the local church. In this system each congregation has a number of elders (including the main teaching pastor), who themselves belong to a "presbytery", which will oversee a group of churches. Some members of each presbytery will in turn belong to a General Assembly which has final authority over all the churches within the denomination. (Some denominations, such as Methodism, function in a similar, though not identical, way to this system.)

3. Independent elder-led. Within the local church, this functions much like a Presbyterian church. But it is not part of a denomination, so the authority resides with the church's elders.

4. Congregational. In this system, it is the congregation itself that is the decision-making authority. Church members will elect officers (such as elders) to lead and run the church. In some cases the church will have one pastor and a number of supporting deacons; in others the pastor will be one of a number of elders overseeing the congregation. Some churches will vote on all matters; others only on the most crucial ones, such as the appointment of a new pastor.

That there are these different forms of church government indicates that this has been an issue over which Christians have had different viewpoints over the years. For some, the particular form of government a church may decide to take is not a major issue to worry about. For others, it is a key point of doctrine. It is for each Christian to determine whether and where they think the Bible is being prescriptive (telling us how to structure our church leadership) or merely descriptive (giving us snapshots of how some of the early churches were led).

What is a pastor meant to do?

While I was training to be a vicar in the Church of England, I went to a friend's fancy-dress party. Lacking imagination (and costumes), I borrowed a friend's clerical collar and went as a clergyman. I got chatting to a group of people I didn't really know, and after a while one of them said, "You're not actually a pastor, are you?" Given I was at that point still a full-time theological student and hadn't started working for a church yet, I replied that I wasn't.

"Thank goodness!" she said (or words to that effect; her language may have been a little more colourful). A sense of relief immediately went round the whole group. No doubt they were thinking about all the things they'd been saying, and whether you'd really want to be saying those things in the presence of a pastor.

"So what do you do?" one of them asked.

"Well," I said, "I'm training to be a pastor..."

The conversation ground to a halt.

I don't know what they thought a pastor was like. Clearly it was not someone they would want to have around on social occasions. But it does raise the question: What is a pastor like? What does a pastor do? This is something that matters for pastors (obviously!) but also for every church member. Many a pastor has been crushed by church members expecting more of him, or different things from him, than God does. And on the other hand, many a church has been compromised because a pastor did less than, or different things from, what God requires of a church leader.

Job description

In Acts 20, Paul has been travelling around what is present-day Turkey and Greece and, before he leaves that region, he has one last stop in a place called Miletus, and sends for the elders of the church in nearby Ephesus for one final meeting. As he addresses them for the last time, Paul reflects on his own ministry, and as he does so, he gives us one of the clearest explanations of what a pastor is to do.

So these are the things you need your church leaders to be doing for you—the things you should be praying for them to be doing. When the time comes for a new pastor to be appointed, these are the things to be looking for. But more than that, in outlining the priorities for Christian leaders, what Paul says does not only apply to pastors and elders, but to anyone in any level of Christian leadership. It applies to those running children's groups, or leading Bible studies, to parents in the spiritual leadership of their children, and to all Christians as we recognise our pastoral responsibilities to serve and encourage one another in the local church.

Let's have a look at this "job description":

1. Serve God: "I served the Lord with great humility and with tears and in the midst of severe testing by the plots of my Jewish opponents" (v 19). The word Paul uses for service is more akin to slavery, and this is the foundation of all Christian ministry. Pastors are to be slaves of Christ, and therefore to serve him "with great humility". A pastor's main aim is to make much of Jesus and not of themselves.

2. Teach people: "You know that I have not hesitated to preach anything that would be helpful to you but have taught you publicly and from house to house" (v 20). We need pastors to teach—and not only from the pulpit, but in conversation. Pastors are to teach what is "helpful". This will mean knowing their church members well enough to know what to say, and how to say it. At the same time they are to teach "the whole will of God" (v 27), including the difficult and unpopular parts.

3. Accept the cost: "I only know that in every city the Holy Spirit warns me that prison and hardships are facing me. However, I consider my life worth nothing to me; my only aim is to finish the race and complete the task the Lord Jesus has given me—the task of testifying to the good news of God's grace" (v 23-24). Serving the Lord is certainly not easy, but Paul was prepared to suffer. It will be the same for all who have been given a task by their master, Christ. Just as staffers in the White House serve "at the pleasure of the President," so also Christian leaders are to serve at the pleasure of Christ.

4. *Care deeply about their church:* "Keep watch over yourselves and all the flock of which the Holy Spirit has made you overseers. Be shepherds of the church of God, which he bought with his own blood" (v 28). Ultimately, of course, every local church is God's—and he has purchased his church at an astonishing price: the blood of Jesus Christ. This flock is precious to him. If the church is worth Christ's blood, then it is certainly worth its leaders' labour.

5. *Protect their flock:* Every church is in need of protection. Sheep are extremely vulnerable animals, with no resources of their own with which to fight or flee. The flock is vulnerable to attack:

> After I leave, savage wolves will come in among you and will not spare the flock. Even from your own number men will arise and distort the truth in order to draw away disciples after them.   *v 29-30*

It is not persecution from without that Paul warns against, but false teaching from within. Teaching that distorts the truth is as savage to the church as a ravenous wolf is to unprotected sheep. The Christian leader is to protect the flock from distortions of the truth.

6. *Guard themselves:* "Keep watch over yourselves" (v 28). Passengers on planes are warned, in emergencies, to put oxygen masks on themselves before helping others with theirs. You're not much help to others if you're

struggling yourself. The same is true pastorally. Church leaders are to keep themselves protected from spiritual harm before giving such protection to others.

The heart of the Christian leader's task is the ministry of God's word. As Paul has shown, this will take many forms. It is more than the formal teaching on a Sunday. It includes leading Bible-study groups, one-to-one discipleship, and even going door to door in an effort to share the word of God. Underlying it all is the reality that it is the "word of [God's] grace" that can "build you up" (v 32). The word that encourages us also grows us as God's people.

The discipline issue

It is in this context that the Bible also talks about church discipline. Because a church is made up of sinful people, there will be occasions in the life of a fellowship when it is sadly necessary to discipline individual members. This kind of discipline is like the discipline that takes place in healthy families. It is part of parental wisdom to discipline children appropriately (Proverbs 13 v 24). Similarly, God himself disciplines his children; in fact, it is an expression of his love for them (Hebrews 12 v 6). So it is not surprising that we are to see a similar process at work in God's household.

Jesus outlines how this discipline is to take place:

If your brother or sister sins, go and point out
their fault, just between the two of you. If they
listen to you, you have won them over. But if they
will not listen, take one or two others along, so

that "every matter may be established by the testimony of two or three witnesses." If they still refuse to listen, tell it to the church; and if they refuse to listen even to the church, treat them as you would a pagan or a tax collector.

Matthew 18 v 15-17

Notice, discipline is the responsibility of each member of the church family. If we are aware of a fellow church member sinning, it is for us to appropriately raise it with them. James says as much in his letter:

My brothers and sisters, if one of you should wander from the truth and someone should bring that person back, remember this: whoever turns a sinner from the error of their way will save them from death and cover over a multitude of sins.

James 5 v 19-20

Paul reminds us that this is all to be done "gently" and while keeping watch of ourselves (Galatians 6 v 1).

Jesus anticipates that there will be times when this one-another discipline is insufficient. Knowledge of the sin being committed is to be kept to as small a number as possible. But if the sin persists, it is necessary to involve a wider group, even the church membership as a whole. Jesus also shows us that there may sadly be times when the church needs to implement the ultimate sanction—removing someone from church membership. This is a necessary and last resort. If someone is still refusing to repent, and ignoring church-wide calls to do so, they are effectively living as an unbeliever and it is therefore appropriate for the church to reflect the seriousness of this by treating them as an unbeliever.

In all of this, it is very clear what the overall purpose is. Jesus talks about the individual concerned being "won over" (Matthew 18 v 15); James of them being "brought back" (James 5 v 19); Paul of them being "restored" (Galatians 6 v 1). In each case, the goal is the same: for them to be restored before the Lord and any whom they have sinned against. Sin affects our fellowship with God and one another, and so discipline is to restore what has been disrupted. The purpose of discipline is always ultimately positive: not that we express disapproval or anger, or that we seek to pay someone back for hurt they may have caused others. It is to restore them back into loving fellowship with the church and its Head.

As you've probably realised by now, this chapter is less about why we bother with church (hopefully you need less persuading on this by now!), and more about how we bother with church. And the "led-ness" of God's church means that we can contribute to our church by giving thanks and praying for our leaders; by placing ourselves under, and supporting, the positive discipline of our church; and, in any pastoring role we have (be it crèche, visiting the elderly, leading a Bible study group, or being the senior pastor) by seeking to match the job description that God, through Paul, lays out.

Can't I view my small group as my church?

Many churches run some kind of small-group ministry. Groups of this sort of size (typically ten or so believers) tend to be one of the best contexts for discussion of Scripture, and for sharing needs for support and prayer. During a main Sunday gathering there might not be the same kind of opportunity to interact at this level. Small groups tend to be where some of the most vital "one another" ministry takes place. Relationships are deepened, insights are shared, and problems and difficulties in life are discussed and addressed.

Because of all this, it can be easy for such a group to become the main focus of its members' spiritual lives. The group becomes, in effect, church.

While this is understandable, it is not desirable. Small groups should not become a replacement for the main church meeting. If your small group becomes your church, you are missing out. It is worth noting that in some contexts where there are not many believers, churches are small enough to function much as a small group does. The Bible does not prescribe what size a church must be. What we are discussing here is not whether healthy churches can be small groups of people—they can—but whether small groups can be a substitute for church—they shouldn't be.

Why not? First, because being a whole church family is also a way of demonstrating who it is that God has reconciled to himself. Our small groups do not likely reflect the whole range of ages and backgrounds that are included in the wider church family. But our Sunday gatherings do, and this is significant.

Second, the scope of what a small group can do is hindered precisely because it is a small group. A church is a body made up of many parts, with each part playing a distinct role in the life of the body. Within a small group there will not be the full range of gifts and ministries that are present in the wider church family.

Third, the small group is not led in the way a church is. So it cannot make a final call on an issue of doctrine or behaviour that the recognised leadership of the church is responsible for. It cannot share the Lord's Supper in a way that speaks of the unity of the whole church.

Small groups can therefore be a terrific supplement to the gathered life of the church, but they should never be a replacement for it. We want to be in a church with small groups, not a church of small groups. The main centre of church life is the whole gathering, not the small groupings.

Should pastors and elders only be men?

In the Western world today it is a scandal to most people that we could even ask such a question. Equality between men and women has been hard-won, and any restriction on what a man or a woman can do feels like a step in the wrong direction.

But the majority of Christians around the world and through the centuries have believed that church pastors should be men. That broad consensus alone should give us significant pause. We must not assume that we know more than the vast majority of the universal church. We need to come to Scripture with open minds.

When we do so, we cannot help but notice something: in all the language where Paul is talking about the role and requirements of an elder, he consistently uses male language. An elder is to be "faithful to his wife" (1 Timothy 3 v 2). It is never the other way round. This is not coincidental. There are some Bible-believing Christians who would differ on this, but it seems very clear that, contrary to modern intuition, the New Testament reserves the role of pastor and elders to qualified men.

In his first letter to Timothy, Paul outlines how the local church is to be conducted. As he zeroes in on some specific points for men in particular and women in particular, he says this:

> A woman should learn in quietness and full submission. I do not permit a woman to teach or to assume authority over a man; she must be quiet. For Adam was formed first, then Eve. And Adam was not the one deceived; it was the woman who was deceived and became a sinner. *1 Timothy 2 v 11-14*

It is very important to notice some features of this text.

1. The context is the teaching and learning that is to go on in the church assembly. Paul wants women to learn. That might seem obvious to us, but in Paul's day that was striking; women were frequently excluded from many forms of education. This was not to be so in church. But in the context of the church being taught, Paul makes it very clear that the authoritative, teaching leadership is to be done by

qualified men only. When Paul says that the woman is to be quiet, he is talking specifically about this area of church life. Elsewhere, he assumes women will be involved in praying and other forms of public speech (1 Corinthians 11 v 5). This restriction on women does not apply beyond this sphere.

2. Paul makes a connection between teaching and assuming authority. These are not two unrelated activities arbitrarily singled out by Paul for comment. The chief way a pastor leads a church is through the ministry of the word. The church is led from the pulpit. Teaching the word of God is how authority is expressed and seen. If a pastor is never teaching the church, he is not strictly the one in authority over it.

3. Paul's reason for reserving pastoring and eldership to men is rooted in the events of the creation and the subsequent fall of Adam and Eve. In other words, it is to do with how God intends us to be as men and women. It is not the case that there were particular circumstances at Ephesus that provoked Paul to teach something that he otherwise would not have taught. This reservation of roles exists because of how God has designed men and women to relate. There is a particular shape and structure that exists to this relationship, and one application of this is that the teaching elders of the local church are to be men.

It is worth saying that churches who agree on this basic principle (often called the "complementarian" view) do differ in how they work it out in practice. Some will reserve all Sunday preaching and small-group leadership to men. Others will allow women to take part in these provided it is under the oversight of the overall church leadership. We also need to bear in mind that this is not a question of who is and who is not a Christian; and that this is a very short answer to a very difficult and often emotive question. So it is well worth speaking to your church leaders about the issue, and continuing to read, pray and think about it—a good place to do some more reading is Kevin DeYoung's book *Freedom and Boundaries*.

Why are there so many denominations?

The New Testament makes clear that the church should be united. Jesus said there was to be "one flock and one shepherd" (John 10 v 16). He prayed that all those who would believe in him "may be brought to complete unity" (John 17 v 23). Similarly, Paul pleaded with the church in Corinth "that all of you agree with one another in what you say and that there be no divisions among you, but that you be perfectly united in mind and thought" (1 Corinthians 1 v 10). In the Bible, unity matters.

The unity Jesus spoke about and prayed for is unity that comes through the gospel. Paul urges his readers to "make every effort to keep the unity of the Spirit" (Ephesians 4 v 3). The Spirit has already brought unity; the church is to maintain and express that unity. This unity is therefore not institutional. We mustn't think that if the whole church of God is not part of one huge human organisation, it is not enjoying unity (nor that if there were one organisation, that would represent or guarantee true unity). The unity sought by Jesus and brought by the Spirit is created by the gospel and not by ecclesiastical bodies.

But nor is it static. Paul continues, "Christ himself gave the apostles, the prophets, the evangelists, the pastors and teachers, to equip his people for works of service, so that the body of Christ may be built up until we all reach unity in the faith" (Ephesians 4 v 11-13). So Christian unity in the life of the local church is something we both maintain and attain. It is given to us in Christ, and we must grow up in it.

So, since unity is so important, why are there so many denominations? Many of the most significant splits within the church have come about as a result of disagreement. For its first 1,000 years, the church enjoyed considerable visible and organisational unity. In AD 1054 what became the Orthodox Church in the east broke away from the Catholic Church in the west over a change a pope had made to a church creed. In the sixteenth century, the Reformation saw the institutional western church separate over a number of fundamental doctrinal issues into Protestant and Roman Catholic branches. In the years following this, the Protestant churches themselves formed into hundreds of further groupings. Today surveys estimate there are 45,000 denominations, compared to just 1,600 in 1900.

Undoubtedly, a huge amount of this is the result of sin. Churches and movements have been formed because of personality clashes, church politics, pride, power and envy. As we look over church history and see such dynamics playing out, we mustn't just shrug at it as if Christians then were far less enlightened than we are now, or accept division as inevitable. We must pray and work for unity around the gospel.

Clearly, too, a certain amount of this organisational splintering was sadly necessary. When a whole denomination or movement slides into false teaching, heeding no calls to repent and return, our own spiritual safety as well as the witness of the gospel requires that we separate from them. There have been times when Christians have bravely stood against falsehood, and as a result new movements have arisen, not least at the time of the Reformation.

Lastly, there is the issue of cults, which are very different to denominations. Cults, generally speaking, exhibit three hallmarks: unbiblical teaching that results in a wrong view of who Jesus is; an exclusivist view (that is, a cult tends to see itself as the only true "church", and anyone not in their group is therefore not saved); and a very domineering leadership structure (often cults are begun by a leader with a magnetic personality). Examples of cults that have formed as a result of deviating from Christianity are The Church of Jesus Christ of Latter-Day Saints (the Mormons), the Jehovah's Witnesses, and the Church of Christ Scientist.

It is important to recognise cults for what they are. But ultimately, if we strive to maintain the Spirit-given unity of faith in God's Son, revealed in his word, then that's what matters—and it's what protects us from error, be it the error of a cult or of a whole institution. Christ will build and protect his church.

Chapter 5

How do I survive church?

There's a sense in which church is meant to be hard work. It is made up of imperfect people. It is not driven by self-interest. Its mission and character are meant to go against the grain of how things normally work in this world. In fact, the very things that make church hard work are often the things that make it great. Think about what these words call us to:

> Do nothing out of selfish ambition or vain conceit. Rather, in humility value others above yourself, not looking to your own interests but each of you to the interests of the others.
>
> *Philippians 2 v 3-4*

Hard work, for sure. It takes effort to not be selfish, to value others' needs above our own and to put the rest of the congregation before ourselves. It goes against every one of our default settings to be like this to others, and it also goes against everyone else's to be like this to you. None of this comes naturally to any of us. Any church is a collection of sinners—saved sinners, but still sinners—and so no local church is going to be perfect. The only perfect church is the heavenly assembly, and this does not meet at 10.30am each Sunday a short drive from your house. So until you're called to join the throng around God's throne, you're called to belong to a church in which others will get things wrong—and so will you.

Sticking with church—loving it and serving it—is often going to be the harder option than either just leaving it, or turning up but not really getting stuck in. How do you survive church? In this chapter we're going to look at three imperfections in our churches that often become reasons why Christians switch off in their church or leave it altogether. They may be the reasons why you've done so or are thinking of doing so.

Church is boring

If we're honest, most churches are quite odd. In my church, there is a huge, gold-plated lectern that's shaped as an eagle. It's called "Percy", takes three grown men to lift, and is used for doing the Bible readings from. It is common in our denomination to have one (though possibly less common to call it Percy), and I forget what it's meant to signify.

More than once, the first reaction of newcomers to the church has been to ask (with some bewilderment) why we have a giant gold eagle at the front of church. I'm so used to it that I don't notice Percy any more. It is much the same with most of the things that are strange about our churches.

Take the sermons. A major part of our services is a monologue. The only other context I can think of where 21st-century people voluntarily listen to a substantial monologue in their leisure time is when they watch stand-up comedy. And it's fair to say most of our preaching is (for better as well as for worse) not much like listening to 90 minutes of Jerry Seinfeld or Michael McIntyre.

Add to this that either side of these monologues might be a hymn that uses Victorian language, and taken as a package it is not hard to see why some people might find church boring. It is not what many of us are used to, unless we've grown up going to church.

There are, sometimes, reasons why you might find church legitimately boring. It's possible for preaching to be based on a Bible text, but to be dull. It's possible for church music to be a dirge, even while the words of the hymns are joyful and exciting. We can be doing the right things, but in a very dull way.

Such reasons exist, but I don't think that's why most of us tend to find church boring. It might just be that we don't find the right sort of things interesting.

Think about it. What do you think is actually going on at your church on a typical Sunday morning? Often we do not see past the surface level: Gladys is on the piano this week, Geoff is preaching on Leviticus, and the coffee is weak again. But if we scratch beneath the surface, something truly remarkable is actually taking place. Jesus promised that:

> Where two or three gather in my name, there am I with them.	*Matthew 18 v 20*

For all its faults and idiosyncrasies, your church is still a community that God has gathered and in which he is present by his Spirit. If the idea of that is boring, then the problem might be with us and not with church. Perhaps we're just interested in the wrong things.

As well as asking what we think is going on, we need to ask why we actually come along. As we've seen, the writer of the letter to the Hebrews recognises the temptation to give up going to church—and he commands his readers to resist that temptation:

> Let us consider how we may spur one another on towards love and good deeds, not giving up meeting together, as some are in the habit of doing, but encouraging one another.
> *Hebrews 10 v 24-25*

Notice what he doesn't say. The focus is not primarily on what we do or don't get out of attending our church, but on what we can give to others. Church is not there for your entertainment, as a consumer, but for you and others to find encouragement, as a contributor. If our "boring-ometer" for church is based on whether we sang songs we liked, or whether the sermon was relevant enough or short enough, or scratching where we have been itching this week, then it could be a sign that we're going to church for our sake and not for the sake of others. A lot of our experience of church has to do with the mindset with which we arrive week by week.

There is a balance here, of course. The preacher does need to be thinking through the points of application of his text that week and considering the various kinds of people who will be listening. The music does need to be a good reflection of the cultural diversity that the church represents and is wanting to reach. It might well be that these things are not being thought about as fully as they might be.

But we do need to examine ourselves, and ask not just whether the ministry team is doing all that they're meant to be doing, but whether as church members we are doing all that we are meant to be doing. It is almost impossible to overstate the positive impact we can have on others if we are coming looking for ways in which to be an encouragement. If that is one of our main goals, then there is every possibility that we can come home from church each week excited, rather than bored.

It is not all one way. And none of this is necessarily going to happen overnight. But if we regularly feel bored by church, it is worth asking whether at least part of it this down to the fact that we have forgotten what is going on as we meet as church, or forgotten why we ourselves turn up to church.

There is one other crucial thing we need to check: are we praying regularly for our church? The answer to that question is a good indication of whether we're coming as Christians, or as consumers.

Church has hurt me

Church can hurt. In fact, if you're in a church for long enough, it *will* hurt. This might range from an unkind comment from someone else, to being seriously let down by someone you trusted, all the way through to being abused by someone else within church. If you are reading this and you have been abused by someone you trusted and had every right to expect to be trustworthy, then I understand why you may well have given up going to church and have no intention of ever going back. Later in this section, I'll make a few suggestions to you, but I don't want you to hear me suggesting that what has happened to you isn't serious. You might need to put this book down and speak to someone you do trust about what has happened.

For most of us, though, our experience of being burned in church is lower level than that, though still hurtful. It could be that we've been hurt by poor leadership. Of course, no pastor or elder will be perfect. The Chief Shepherd of the church is flawless but his undershepherds are not, and sometimes they will be much less than perfect.

Perhaps it was leadership that was domineering and bullying. Or leadership that was ineffectual and unsupportive. Or leadership that did not continue to hold to the truth of the Bible. Or leadership that was insensitive. I think of a couple I know who have been unable to conceive children, or someone I know who has been single long-term, or someone I know who has been recently bereaved, all of whom have been hurt at some point by a flippant comment made by a pastor during a sermon. I have been hurt myself. I know there have been times, as a pastor, when I have unwittingly said something insensitive, and am grateful for patient church members pointing this out when it has been the case.

It could be that we've been hurt by other church members. Again, we are all sinful, and sometimes our sin will hurt someone else. It might be that someone betrayed a confidence, or let us down in some way. Or a brother or sister has been, frankly, vindictive to us, either as a one-off or as a pattern of behaviour.

Our instinct when we're hurt is to lash out, or run away, or perhaps to grin and bear it and pretend it doesn't matter. None of these are effective ways of responding. When wrong has been done there needs to be repentance and forgiveness. Both are necessary. But they don't necessarily rely on each other—it's easy to make your forgiveness conditional on someone saying sorry; equally we can hold off from saying sorry because the other person doesn't seem ready to say it's OK.

As we have already seen, Jesus himself knew his church would be a place where hurts would be caused—and gave us a roadmap on how to deal with it:

> If your brother or sister sins, go and point out their fault, just between the two of you. If they listen to you, you have won them over.
>
> *Matthew 18 v 15*

Often, we just don't do this. We allow resentment and bitterness to grow within us, and that can become a more serious sin than whatever kicked it off in the first place. It is all too easy to fester, continue to fester, and then to explode. These things need to be nipped in the bud—we need to give the person who hurt us the opportunity to see the effect of their actions, to say sorry, and to change. We need churches where we are willing to say, and to hear, "Friend, I'm feeling hurt by what you did… Can we talk about it and pray about it?"

And then we need to be willing to forgive. Tim Keller once defined forgiveness as resolving not to bring the offence up again with God, with the person who offended us, or with ourselves. Often it is the final one of these that is the most difficult.

Sometimes, there may be no apparent way to resolve the issue. The church may be at fault in not seeking to help or to discipline. Sadly, there may be no means of moving on without leaving. But I would want to caution that leaving the church must be the absolute last resort, not the first option. Remember that leaving a church means cutting yourself off from your family, removing yourself from the body you belong to. And make sure you are not just leaving, but also joining— that you know which church you are going to move to, which body you are going to serve.

Lastly, let me add a word or two to anyone who is not going to church because you've been so hurt by church in the past. First, I'm so glad you're reading this—that you're willing, however provisionally at this stage, to consider giving church another go. Second, we need to be realistic. You are not going to go from "0-60" quickly. You're not going to get everything fixed up and ready for this Sunday morning. It may take you a long time to learn that you can trust people again if in a previous church you have been badly hurt.

The journey back to church will need to be done gently and slowly—but at the same time, you do need to be up for making that journey. You need a church, and there's a church out there that needs you. Perhaps you could speak to a trusted Christian friend who is at a church near you, and work out a way you can begin that journey, even in small steps. It might be that the appropriate first step for you is to slip into the service just after it starts and slip out again before it finishes, if you need to. It might be that you could get used to meeting up to pray with a couple of others who are part of that church before you start going on Sundays.

Whatever steps you take, they will not always be easy. But I hope, on some level at least, that you at least desire to start making them. It would be a great thing to pray for.

Church has exhausted me

Churches can all too easily end up amassing people who used to be full of zeal, and now are full of disappointment. It might be that we had great hopes for a particular ministry and yet are now just demoralized, tired, and wondering why anyone bothers. Maybe we're tired of being asked to do more than we can bear. We might feel that our efforts are unappreciated, or make no difference, or are never enough. We were on fire; now we're burned out.

To survive (and maybe even thrive) in church, it's

necessary to keep two realities simultaneously in our minds: what the church is humanly and what it is spiritually. Doing this enables us to be hopeful and ambitious, all the while remaining realistic. We need to avoid both cynicism and naivety.

Humanly, the church is a group of very flawed people who meet regularly on Sundays and through the week. People do not generally change very quickly. People make mistakes and there are tensions and disagreements. There are difficult characters. Not much would look immediately impressive to a first-time visitor.

Spiritually, the church is a group that God has gathered together to himself and to each other. Despite even vast socio-economic or cultural differences that might exist between them, they are bound together by something that transcends anything this world can rally around.

So in church, there is real community and sharing of life. There are people who have been quietly and gradually drawn to Christ. There are people who have been quietly and gradually healed of deep wounds. These people, for all their quirks, meet together to celebrate all that God has shown himself to be to them and to showcase his grace to a watching world. All that this church is and does cannot be ultimately accounted for by the usual measurements of this world. God is undeniably present and at work.

If we only take the human view, we'll become cynical. If we only remember the spiritual view, we'll become naïve. Either way, we'll become disillusioned. So we have to learn to look at our church as Paul looked at the Corinthian church. This was a church he had planted; a church he had pastored; a church he had given years to. But by the time he wrote his first letter to them, it was a total mess. It was divided, proud, immoral and theologically wobbly. Paul could even say to them, "Your meetings do more harm than good" (1 Corinthians 11 v 17). It's hard to imagine a church so bad that it would be better off not having Sunday services! Things were in serious disarray. From a human view, we'd expect Paul to be totally demoralised.

But he isn't, because, as he reminds the Corinthians, despite all their huge flaws and failings, they are still...

> ... the church *of God* in Corinth ... *sanctified* in Christ Jesus and called to be his holy people.
>
> *1 v 2 (my emphasis)*

They are horribly sinful, but they are also sanctified—pure and Christ-like—in God's sight, through their faith in Jesus. And so Paul, without ignoring how much of a mess this church is, says:

> I always thank my God for you because of his grace given you in Christ Jesus.   *1 v 4*

He views this church from both a human and a spiritual view, so he's realistic about them but not demoralized by them; ambitious for them but not surprised by their sin. They are a mess, but they are God's mess, and Paul knows that straightening out messes like this are something of a speciality for God.

And so here is something of a survival kit for your

imperfect and flawed, yet precious and God-dwelled church. Remember who is there as you meet, and why you are there—and church will never be boring. Seek to be patient, to lovingly confront and completely forgive when you are hurt—and you'll be able to survive being sinned against. Hold together the human and spiritual view of your church—and you'll remain both realistic and ambitious.

After all, your church is a miracle. Next Sunday, look at those sitting around you. It's amazing that they're there. It's amazing that they're still trusting Jesus this Sunday—another week of God's grace to them. It's amazing that you're there, trusting Jesus this Sunday—another week of God's grace to you. And it's amazing that you, with all your differences and sometimes disagreements, are sitting in the same room, serving the same God and encouraging each other—a wonderful visual aid of God's grace to his people. Your church is imperfect. And that makes your church all the more miraculous. Its imperfections are in themselves exciting, because they show just how powerful and loving the God who has brought you together must be.

Chapter 6

How can I be a good church member?

Church is not something we go to but something we belong to.

Some churches will have formal membership schemes where joining involves completing a membership process of some sort and making commitments to the church. Others do not. But either way, we are to see ourselves as members of our local church, not just attendees or supporters:

> In Christ we, though many, form one body, and each member belongs to all the others.
>
> *Romans 12 v 5*

You belong to the other members of your church family. You are a member of the body of Christ and you express that membership by belonging to the body of his local church.

What we are beginning to see, then, is that the answer to the question, "Why should I bother with church?" necessarily raises the question, "How should I bother with church?"—what does it mean in practice to belong to my church family? How do I love the people Jesus has loved enough to die for?

Attending

The most obvious way to express our membership of a church family is by committing to being there regularly and making weekly attendance a priority—at midweek groups as well as on Sundays. We show up. We're determined to. We won't just be there when we happen to be in town with nothing else on. We'll be there when it inconveniences us. We'll be prepared to cut a weekend trip short to be back in time for church. We'll go when the weather's bad. We'll go when we're tired and would rather have the time to ourselves. We recognise that we need this kind of fellowship and encouragement every single week of our lives, even when we're really not in the mood for it.

I will do this if I've realised something crucial: going to church is not about me and what I'll get out of it this week. I belong to the others there, and so it is about them and how I can encourage and serve them. This shifts my focus. I'm not now thinking, "Is church going to scratch where I itch today? If not, maybe I will give it a miss." No, I'll be thinking, "I need to be with my Christian family today. I need the rest of the body, and the rest of the body needs me."

It is hard to get to know the rest of my church family and for them to get to know me if I am not attending regularly. It is hard for me to be led by those God has placed over me if I only show up occasionally. The most fundamental way in which we express our membership of a church is by being there.

Involvement

As well as physically being at church week by week, we need to be actively involved in the life of our congregation. We need to be aware of what is going on, what the needs are and what issues are facing the church at the moment. If our church has meetings specifically for church members to be aware of what's going on and to have input into decisions that are facing the church, we need to be there and taking part. If it is our church we should (a) know what is going on, and (b) have a stake in that.

Praying

We need to pray for the life of our church in a way that is informed and regular. We need to be at the prayer meeting, where particular needs and news are shared. We need to use whatever prayer bulletin is provided for church members. We need to pray for the missionaries sent out by the church. And we need to pray for our fellow church members (just as we need them to pray for us).

If your church has a members' directory, this can be a great fuel for prayer. Quite apart from the good it does them to have us praying for them, it also has a wonderful effect on us. Nothing helps us feel that we belong to a body of people more than regularly praying for them. Unfamiliar names become familiar, and we find that the more we pray for people, the more we find ourselves caring for them. If you've never really felt as if you've belonged at your church, try praying for the other members, by name and regularly.

There are a number of ways you can go about doing this. You might pray for a set number of people each day or each week. Even in a church of a few hundred, you will find that you get through the entire list before too long. If you belong to a multi-congregational or multi-site church, then perhaps focus your prayers on those who belong to the same congregation as you.

Serving

Belonging to a church family means that we put the needs of others there before our own. As Paul said to the church in Philippi, we must...

> ... do nothing out of selfish ambition or vain conceit. Rather, in humility value others above yourselves, not looking to your own interests but each of you to the interests of the others.
>
> *Philippians 2 v 3-4*

In doing so, the church body is simply following the example of its Head, Jesus (v 5). We need to serve our church family.

God has given gifts to every member of the body of Christ precisely so that they can serve the body and help to build it up:

> Now to each one the manifestation of the Spirit is given for the common good.   *1 Corinthians 12 v 7*

Each of us will have been given ways of being a blessing to our church family. We need to find out what the needs are in our church and think about where and how we might be able to help. To mangle the famous comment by JFK, we are to ask not what our church can do for us, but what we can do for our church.

Giving

One of the ways in which we express our being part of a church family is by having a financial stake in it. It is one of the ways that most solidifies our commitment—we are literally invested in the work when we are giving our money to it. Giving financially to the ministry of your church is a way of directing your heart there:

> Where your treasure is, there your heart will be also.   *Matthew 6 v 21*

If you have never felt that you truly cherish your church, it may be because you've never really given sacrificially to its needs.

There's another reason for giving—Paul says that it is right for churches to financially support their pastors:

> The one who receives instruction in the word should share all good things with their instructor.
> *Galatians 6 v 6*

To his young protégé Timothy he wrote:

> The elders who direct the affairs of the church
> well are worthy of double honour, especially
> those whose work is preaching and teaching …
> "The worker deserves his wages."
>
> *1 Timothy 5 v 17-18*

Giving regularly is a discipline, and one it does us good to develop. You may have extremely limited financial resources. But even giving a small amount each month or each year will grow you in the discipline of giving, and also gives us the joy of being invested in the Lord's work in this way. Paul describes giving as a "grace" (2 Corinthians 8 v 7); if we don't give at all, we're the ones who will miss out the most.

Submitting

The writer to the Hebrews tells us:

> Have confidence in your leaders and submit to
> their authority, because they keep watch over
> you as those who must give an account. Do this
> so that their work will be a joy, not a burden, for
> that would be of no benefit to you.
>
> *Hebrews 13 v 17*

Many of us live in cultures that are increasingly suspicious and resentful of authority. We may be aware of how little secular leaders have our best interests at heart. The idea of someone having spiritual authority over us, still worse of our submitting to that authority, does not naturally sit well with us. Yet this is how God has designed us to flourish as his people: to have leaders over us that we are to honour and submit to.

This does not mean we'll agree with everything they say. But if our church has policies on certain things then, provided those policies do not contradict Scripture, we are to submit to those policies. We do this recognising that church leaders are accountable to God for how they watch over us. They should not take that role lightly, and therefore nor should we.

Our respectful submission to their authority will make their work joyful and not burdensome, and that in turn will be a blessing to us. We're allowed to disagree and we're allowed to thrash issues out in respectful discussion. But we are called by God to submit to our leaders. And if we only submit when we agree with them or when it suits us, we are not allowing ourselves to be led by them, which means we're not really letting ourselves be led by God.

Remember, faithful pastoral ministry is hard work, and pastors need to be encouraged by their church members. The best way is to pray regularly for them. It makes the world of difference to me to know that there are particular members of my church who pray for me and our ministry every day. So pray for your pastor often, and drop him a line to let him know. Saturday evenings can be an especially crucial time. There may still be work to be done on the sermon (sermons are never really finished—much like books, they can always be improved!), or apprehension over a difficult situation that needs dealing with the next day, or last-minute changes being made to the service if someone has pulled out. Saturday is a great day to pray for your pastor, your church, and yourself as you prepare to meet with God's people.

It is also the responsibility of church members to make sure their pastor is being well looked after and cared for. As we've seen, churches are to support their pastor financially. But there is also a need to make sure they have a healthy work-life balance, spending enough time with family and friends. Many pastors are prone to overwork—there is always more that needs doing.

We also need to remember that pastors are church members too. They need the same pastoral care as anyone else. They will have battles in their Christian life. I remember one church member being quite shocked when I told her I was going through a period of struggling with my devotional life. We need to let our pastors be Christians, not putting them on any kind of pedestal and assuming that the Christian life just happens automatically for them, but getting alongside them, encouraging and supporting and loving them.

Devotion

If there is a word that sums all this up, it is devotion. We have already seen this. When Luke gave his sketch of the early Christian church in Acts 2, this was the adjective he used: "They devoted themselves" to being taught, to one another in fellowship, and to drawing close to God together in prayer. These were not aspects of church life they were just approving of. They even go beyond cold commitment. It was a matter of the heart—they were devoted.

This sounds rather like hard work, and it is. Devotion is not a laid-back, feet-up-on-the-couch kind of word. It speaks of spending ourselves—using our time, giving our gifts, investing our emotions. But it speaks of doing so gladly, because in God's church we find something worth being devoted to—an embassy of God's kingdom, a family of God's people, the bride of the Lord Jesus. It is remembering what the church is, and whose the church is, that makes hard work glad work, and keeps us joyfully devoted.

When the apostle John wrote his first letter to the churches under his care, he repeatedly used affectionate language. They were not just his colleagues; they were his beloved (1 John 2 v 1). And they were his beloved because they were Christ's beloved. Once we grasp Christ's deep affection for the church, we cannot help but begin to share it. We become devoted.

What is the future of the church?

As much of the Western world becomes more secular, it is fashionable to forecast the demise of organised religion in general, and of Christianity in particular. Declining church attendance in some quarters is often cited as an indication that the church is on the way out.

It's true that a number of mainstream Christian denominations are experiencing huge falls in membership. But to a large extent, this decline has accompanied growing theological liberalism. Bible-believing churches have been somewhat healthier numerically. Not all the church is in decline everywhere. As someone recently observed on Twitter, saying the church is in decline is like saying it's raining in Asia: always true somewhere, but never true everywhere.

But, more importantly, the Bible makes several promises about the future of the church:

Growth. Jesus said, "I will build my church, and the gates of Hades will not overcome it" (Matthew 16 v 18). Jesus is very clear: the church is his ongoing building project. His intention is to grow and strengthen it. It is not going away any time soon.

Hardship. There will always be opposition from surrounding culture, temptations from within the church, and the devil standing behind it all. Jesus reminds us that the world hated him and so it will not be unusual for it to hate his people also (John 15 v 18). The church will grow, but life for the church will not be easy.

Glory. The final glimpse we have of the church in the Bible comes right at the end: "I saw the Holy City, the new Jerusalem, coming down out of heaven from God, prepared as a bride beautifully dressed for her husband" (Revelation 21 v 2). The church is spoken of as a society of people perfected by heaven and utterly enthralled by Jesus Christ. Whatever ups and downs might come in the years ahead for particular congregations and denominations, this is the ultimate future of the church!

What's really going on?

No one in the park I walked through seemed to notice me as I walked past them, Bible tucked under my arm. They probably didn't know that there was a church service about to begin. Our entire meeting went on without them being aware.

But someone was watching what we did. Quite a lot of someones, in fact, because...

> Through the church, the manifold wisdom of God
> [is] made known to the rulers and authorities
> in the heavenly realms, according to his eternal
> purpose that he accomplished in Christ Jesus our
> Lord. *Ephesians 3 v 10-11*

When God's people gather, the spiritual world is watching. Though you can't see it, when you meet this Sunday, the spiritual powers—both those loyal to God and those who oppose him—will look on. And they won't notice what either impresses or disappoints us about our church. They won't be struck by the stage and sound system, the parking lot and the band; or the broken heating, the peeling paint, weak orange juice and the struggling organ.

They'll be struck instead by who is meeting there—that such diverse people are sitting together and loving each other because they know that the Lord Jesus loves them and died for them. The church is the way in which God showcases his wisdom to the spiritual realms. It is how he demonstrates the power and the beauty of the gospel. Nothing else in the universe can fuse such varied people together into a new humanity. Only the person and work of Jesus can do this. When the church gathers to worship—whether in Dallas or Dubai, Durham or Delhi—the supremacy of Christ is once again being placarded across the spiritual realms.

Why bother with church? Because it's the most important show in town. What goes on when a church meets is far grander than we tend to realise.

It's God's family.

It's God's embassy in this world.

It's God's way of preaching to the spiritual world.

It is, amazingly, Jesus' bride, who will live with him in the next world.

And, in God's great mercy, through faith in Christ, you get to be a part of it and to be part of the way God builds it. And if you remember this when you get up next Sunday, you'll find yourself asking: *Why on earth would I* **not** *bother with church?*

thegoodbook
COMPANY
Opening up the Bible

At The Good Book Company, we are dedicated to helping Christians and local churches grow. We believe that God's growth process always starts with hearing clearly what he has said to us through his timeless word—the Bible.

Ever since we opened our doors in 1991, we have been striving to produce resources that honour God in the way the Bible is used. We have grown to become an international provider of user-friendly resources to the Christian community, with believers of all backgrounds and denominations using our Bible studies, books, evangelistic resources, DVD-based courses and training events.

We want to equip ordinary Christians to live for Christ day by day, and churches to grow in their knowledge of God, their love for one another, and the effectiveness of their outreach.

Call us for a discussion of your needs or visit one of our local websites for more information on the resources and services we provide.

Your friends at The Good Book Company

UK & EUROPE
NORTH AMERICA
AUSTRALIA
NEW ZEALAND

thegoodbook.co.uk
thegoodbook.com
thegoodbook.com.au
thegoodbook.co.nz

0333 123 0880
866 244 2165
(02) 6100 4211
(+64) 3 343 2463

WWW.CHRISTIANITYEXPLORED.ORG
Our partner site is a great place for those exploring the Christian faith, with a clear explanation of the good news, powerful testimonies and answers to difficult questions.